Contents

I had my own notion of grief
I thought it was the sad time
That followed the death of someone you love
And you had to push through it
To get to the other side

But I'm learning that there is no other side
There is no pushing through
But rather
There is Absorption
Adjustment
Acceptance

And grief is not something you complete
But rather you endure
Grief is not a task to finish
And move on
But an element of yourself
An alteration of your being
A new way of seeing
A New Definition of Self.

~Gwen Flowers
Written in honor of her babies: Skyler, Jordan,
Hannah, Hope and Nicholas

WHAT DO I WEAR THE SECOND YEAR?

There was a time when a widow was expected to wear black clothing for a year after her husband died. This showed her respect and love for him and alerted everyone that she was in grief. The problem with this practice was—what happened when the year was over? There was nothing designed to let the world know that she was still in pain over the death. It was assumed that grief suddenly ended on the first anniversary of his death and she was thought to be back to "normal." I can only imagine how glad she was to get rid of those black dresses. But, I can also imagine how many times she wanted to shout, "But I still hurt!" when the magic one year day arrived.

Almost every grieving person I have known has, at some time, said that the second year of their grief was harder than the first in some ways. Most have expressed surprise at that and have wondered why it was so. When I speak about grief beyond the first year, people are often shocked that there even needs to be a discussion about that. Somehow we have a built-in idea that grief lasts one year and then. . . it is over.

This idea seems to be pervasive in our history. While a woman was wearing black, it was just understood that she was not to look at another man for that year. I can't find any such restrictions placed

> *Grieving is a necessary passage and a difficult transition to finally letting go of sorrow—it is not a permanent rest stop.*
> ~Dodinsky

on the men of that day, but then women were the only ones allowed to grieve. Men were to be "real" men and suck it up and get on with their lives.

How Long?

Some religious practices through the centuries have developed very specific guidelines for the appropriate way to grieve and the timelines within which to grieve. The *one-year* idea might have come from the customs of grieving which have very specific and prescribed time frames and activities that are supposed to take place.

In the Jewish tradition, Aninut is the period from the moment of death until burial. The first week after the funeral is known as Shiva, the seven days of intense mourning. The next stage of the mourning process is known as Shloshim, a 30-day period from the day of the funeral. Shnat ha-evel, the first year of mourning, is reserved only for those who have lost parents during which the Kaddish is to be repeated daily. It is customary in some communities to keep the tombstone veiled, or to delay in putting it up, until the end of the 12-month mourning period.

In the Muslim faith the grieving period is identified as lasting for three days. For a woman whose spouse has died, she experiences the eddah, which lasts four months and 10 days.

In the Hindu tradition there are 13 days of official mourning.

Roman Catholics are expected to pray for and mourn their dead for a year.

So the basic message that grieving individuals receive from society, from history, from religious tradition, from common practice is—grieving is all over the map. The times set aside and the people for whom we are supposed to mourn varies widely.

Wherever the idea of the one-year period of mourning came from, the prevailing idea is that we should be "well" after one year and, when that doesn't happen, we are left wondering if there is something wrong with us. Since there is no standard for grief and everyone grieves in their own way and on their own schedule, we are all left wondering if we are doing it right. The second year is coming and we are still caught up in our loss which really brings on the self-doubt and fear that we are not doing our grieving in the right way.

The First Year: Grieving Interrupted

I really think that the more intentional and focused grieving, and most of the healing, happens after the first year. Somewhere toward the end of the first year is when most folks really begin facing the reality of their loss and begin to deal with the more specific losses. The first year we are so enmeshed in the pain and are just trying to survive. The grief comes in waves that overwhelm us and all we can do is shed tears and hurt. The capacity to think or respond is buried in the pain.

We are also far too busy in the first year. There are so many demands put upon us to take care of the business issues. Too many bills to pay, lawyers to visit, wills to be dealt with, and families to please, for there to be very much time for us to actually just grieve. We grieve on the run. We grieve in spurts between interruptions.

The first year forces us to deal with a seemingly endless number of "firsts." The first holidays after the death, the first birthday, the first anniversary of marriage in the case of the death of a spouse. Endless first things missed after a child dies. And then comes the first anniversary of the death. All of these bring a new wave of pain and dominate our lives with a desperate struggle to survive. The pain, the waves of grief, the firsts, and the demands all make the grief journey one of starts and detours during the first days, weeks and months of the journey.

To add to this blur, we are numb. The mind protects itself from going crazy and just shuts down. It sounds like a contradiction, but we can hurt and be numb at the same time. The depression of grief does not exemplify itself with just sad feelings. It also brings no feelings. We feel detached as though we are outside of ourselves, watching us go through the motions of life, but not being emotionally involved ourselves.

This numbness makes it harder to actually deal with the intense part of grieving during the first year. As the feelings return, usually in the second year, we are often surprised at how much we still hurt and how many new hurts we discover.

All of these factors make it very hard to find the time or the emotional capacity to face all of the ramifications grief brings to our lives. It is unrealistic to think this can be done in one year or in any set period of time. As Yogi Bera said, "It ain't over 'til it's over", and no one can put a time limit on how long it should take.

Unfortunately it seems that most of the material about grief and nearly all of the help we receive in our grief journey is offered during the first year when we can receive it the least. Grief groups are usually full of people in the early stages of the journey. Friends gradually fade way and stop calling and often start avoiding us. We must get accustomed to seeing them dart down the other aisle of the grocery store to avoid having to say anything to us. They have run out of platitudes and don't know what else to say. Churches are quite often content with helping until the funeral is over and then feeling like their job is done. The family seems intent on getting back to business as usual as soon as possible, and the whole world thinks, "It has been a year, shouldn't this be finished now?" Then comes the second year, and the years beyond.

THE SPECIFICS OF GRIEF

It needs to be understood that when we refer to the first year, and the second year or years beyond, we are not talking about set calendar periods. Everyone moves at their own pace and these changes can happen earlier or later. The point is it is almost like we deal with the big picture of grief during the early period after a death—grief in general or the overall view of the process. Gradually we begin to deal with the more specific losses and hurts.

I have written a great deal about what I call the inventory of grief. We do not know what we have lost until we lose it. We do not really know the value of a loved one until they are gone. It is almost like we must inventory the loss before we can grieve it. That inventory takes much longer than one would expect. Discovering someone's true worth takes time.

At first we are constantly thinking of something we wanted to ask the loved one or something we wanted to do with them or for them. It is the process of facing the reality of the loss. If we had to face it all at once, it would be far too much to bear. In time, the inventory becomes more specific and we remember experiences, touches and, increasingly, how much they actually meant in our lives. Those are the kinds of issues we deal with beyond the first period, which might be the first year.

Even if happiness forgets you a little bit, never completely forget about it.
~Jacques Prévert

My wife died four years ago. I think the third anniversary of her death was harder for me than the second because the inventory was more complete and I

❖ 11 ❖

knew a lot more about what I had lost and what I would never have again.

The purpose of this book is not to set dates or times for anything to happen. It is an effort to give permission for grief to continue happening as long as necessary and to allow each person to feel normal in that process. Please understand when I talk of first year or second year that is just a convenient way to say that it takes longer than most people think. And the second year is also not a magic number. It just means longer than the first and can stretch as long as needed.

Transitions

I don't believe that grief has set stages we must walk through, but I do think there are transitions in grief. We seem to go from the time of blinding pain, time consuming details, shock and numbness, to a time of reaction and questioning. We begin to hear ourselves saying a lot of *What ifs, If onlys* and *I should haves.* It is like we came out of a fog and started demanding some answers. These issues have been there all the time and had often crowded their way into our minds, but the crush of time and the overwhelming pain tended to make them hit and fade away.

During the early days of grief our minds are whirling so fast we cannot dwell on anything for very long. I remember thinking that I would never see my wife again, only to have some other thought crowd in and the deep and painful reality of that thought did not become real to me. As time passes all of those passing thoughts start to land in our minds and do not go away. They become reality to us and become the basis of the grief journey now. So the fleeting "I will never see her again," becomes the all night reality that lands on the chest and won't go away.

During the early days after my wife died, if someone asked me what I missed I would answer, "Everything. I just miss her. I miss her presence." Today I would say I miss the sense of security from hearing her soft snore in the night and knowing she was okay. I miss hearing her shuffle down the hall on feet so crippled from arthritis no one but her would dare walk on them. I miss feeling like we were made out of Legos® and only

complete when we were plugged in to each other, the long talks
with someone whose mind seemed to be in sync with mine so
completely that we could complete each other's thoughts.

There were feelings and senses that cannot be explained
nor even described. When we embraced it felt like I was being
refueled with something I could not describe. I thought of it like
an airplane connecting with a tanker plane and being fueled,
but it was more mystical than that. Some mysterious energy
passed between us, an energy I miss but cannot really talk
about, because there are no words nor illustrations that fit. I am
sure others had their own experiences or feelings they cannot
describe and yet that is part of what we lost and certainly part of
what we miss.

I have heard similar responses from parents who have
suffered the death of a child. "If I could just hear him slam the
front door one more time as he came in from play, and smell his
sweaty hair once again." "If I could feel the silk of her hair as I
brushed it over and over and she loved my doing so." They, too,
have feelings about the child that are beyond words. How does
one describe the joy that wells up inside of us while watching
our child having a wonderful time playing with friends? Or the
deep feeling of love while tucking them in at night and realizing
there is no other feeling on earth like that.

I could add an endless list of illustrations but these will
suffice to remind us that gradually grief becomes more and more
specific and each thing remembered becomes a source of our
grief. We do not want a single one of these removed or forgotten.
We simply need help in dealing with them and understanding
how each one impacts our lives. Then these individual losses can
be gathered together into some of our fondest memories and
cherished forever.

GRIEF'S IMPACT

Dealing with grief involves more than the intense pain and loneliness. At some point during the journey we begin to deal with the drastic changes in our lives. Some call this discovering a new normal. We may not have noticed during the time of blinding intensity but, in so many ways, our lives will never be the same. Since the impact of every loss is unique to each individual and varies with the type of loss we can only list enough to suggest the types of impacts. We need to look at the death of a spouse, the death of a child and the death by suicide separately.

The Death Of A Spouse

The death of a mate impacts our very life style. We lose some things we can never replace and must face some decisions we never dreamed we would face.

A New Identity

This is sometimes more prevalent in women than in men, especially people of my generation, but many people wake up about the second year and realize they no longer know who they are. Quite often a woman's identity is wrapped up in her husband so intently that, when he is gone, she feels lost as a human being. Often they have never had a chance to build an identity for themselves apart from parents or husbands. They went from being someone's daughter to being someone's wife and usu-

We must embrace pain and burn it as fuel for our journey.
~Kenji Miyazawa

ally never gave any thought to an individual identity. Suddenly they must decide who they are and what kind of person they want to be. This sounds simple, but it is scary. They feel naked and alone with no one to guide or give shelter:

Who am I?

How am I suppose to act?

Who am I responsible to?

Why do I feel so lost?

Sometimes this can be a very healing experience. If a person has been dominated most of their lives, they are now free to be whomever and whatever they choose. But if they have never had that chance, the sudden freedom leaves them feeling vulnerable and alone.

The search for identity is a private battle inside of each person, but nothing would feel much better than having this subject talked about openly among a group of peers. Just knowing someone else feels similar to what we feel is beyond encouraging.

Who Will Take Care of Me?

That thought hits very early after a death, but it hits and runs. It flashes through our minds like a thousand other thoughts and then seems to hang in the back somewhere waiting to really be faced. Then we wake up and, suddenly, it cannot be avoided or postponed:

How am I going to live and who will be there for me?

Who will take care of me if I am ill?

Who will help me understand and face health issues, financial issues, living decisions?

Who will call the plumber?

Many of us have never lived alone and have not made any plans to do so. We think women are more unprepared for this than men, but, in many cases, they can handle it much better than men. Far too many men have no idea how to live alone. They know how to run a lawn mower but, watch them try to load the dishwasher or cook a meal, and it becomes apparent why so many men marry so soon after a wife dies.

Will I Have Enough Money?

A widow with a million dollars in the bank will ask that question. No matter how much is there, we suddenly feel vulnerable and wonder about the future. This is true of those already retired and made more imminent because their income drops when they lose the spouse's income. It certainly hits the young because of all that lies ahead. Financial security is always illusive. We know what income is there but all the money in stocks and IRAs seems almost mythical and unreal. When the spouse was alive and the financial talks could be shared, somehow it felt secure. Alone is a new ball game.

A group in Oklahoma designed a program for churches to minister to the widows in their care. They have visited with me on occasion asking what the program should cover. I suggested that churches form a group of trusted business people to be available to widows for guidance and simply to answer questions. Often they need to just feel secure as they face the future financially alone.

What About Dating and Remarriage?

There was a time when "if you didn't wait a year you did not love your mate." Thankfully that idea passed long ago and there is no set time for dating to begin or marriage to happen. This is such an individualized issue any author would shudder at trying to answer the question. In general, you should date when you feel ready to do so. In specific, there are some issues that color that statement. Don't marry just because you don't know how to live alone. If you feel desperate, wait until you know you don't have to marry.

Watch out for the first few months. When a mate dies, we have a biological urge to find a new mate. That is true of all animals and we are not exceptions. Three weeks after my wife died I woke up wondering who I could marry. I had no intention of remarrying and, yet, I was in a frantic search. I understood that was biological and that it would pass in time, and it did. During that time, we are not ready to make these choices.

And the last suggestion, spend as much time as needed to establish your new identity before trying to choose a mate. Know who you are and what you really want, then look for someone that fits the new you.

This list could go on forever. Suffice it to say that after the first rush of pain and waves of despair comes a time of specific grief and hard questions.

The Loss of A Child

The first months and even years after a child dies are spent in overwhelming grief and sadness. There may not be any deeper hurt than that felt by a grieving parent.

A mother whose daughter had died four years prior to our meeting told me her daughter seemed to ride on her shoulder and live in her heart. She said the sense of her being there gave her great comfort and, even though she could not admit it to her friends, she talked with her daughter a great deal. She held her hand in front of her face and said that right after the death her daughter was constantly in front of her face. Twenty-four hours a day, seven days a week, all she thought of was her daughter. She stopped being a person and became a grieving parent. When someone would ask how she was doing it made her want to shout "Can't you see? She is right there in front of my face!"

Gradually the daughter began to move, slowly at first. The mother would realize some time had passed without thinking of her daughter. That would frighten her and make her feel like she was forgetting, so she would make an effort to put her back in front of her eyes. In time, it became all right for her to move. She said grief is a journey from "sight to sight to heart to heart." It takes a long time and it is extremely painful but, in time, we live with them inside of our hearts.

That is a beautiful analogy of the intense feelings following the death of a child, but what about after that initial journey has taken its toll on us?

There is no footprint too small to leave an imprint on this world.
~Author Unknown

What must we face then? And how do we face it without thinking there is something wrong with us? Shouldn't we be stronger? Are we just wallowing in our grief?

The death of a child shakes the very foundation of our being. It threatens every thing we cling to for security. It challenges every belief system we have known. If my child can be taken, if that can happen, then anything can happen. How can I ever be safe again?

Faith

A child's death shakes whatever faith we might have had. A minister whispered to me after I spoke at a Compassionate Friends meeting, "I have told my parishioners for years that we have angels watching over and guarding us. Where was the angel the night my daughter was killed in a car wreck?" That plea haunted me for months. Not because the angels were not there, but because I knew there was no one or no place that minister could go to talk about that openly. Where do we go when we are no longer sure about God or fairness and justice? Who will just listen and not preach?

Is there anything more natural than asking why? Matter of fact, is there anything more normal than screaming, "Why did this happen to me?" and then having to realize that all of the philosophic or theological answers in the world will not make that question go away?

We are left to struggle with these issues inside of ourselves or, if we are lucky, with one or two very understanding friends or family members. I have bumped into many people along the way who have faced these issues and formed a new normal for their beliefs. One woman said, "When my son died I lost all the magic in my religion. I found a new way to believe that I like better, but it has no magic in it."

Significance

At some point we begin to search for and try to establish some sense of significance to the life. What did this life mean? Was it meaningless? Does any life have meaning? Are we just things that live and die and make no impact?

I discovered the connection between grief and significance when a young woman who had suffered the death of a husband and then, after remarrying, had suffered the death of a child. I have used this explanation in other books, but it just seems to be the perfect way to illustrate what we are searching for.

She was explaining to me the difference between the loss of a spouse and the loss of a child. She said, "The death of a spouse is a process of letting go, of saying goodbye. The death of a child is a process of hanging on, of trying not to say goodbye. You don't feel like the child has lived long enough to establish their *significance* and you must establish it for them; like walking through the world in their skin."

Significance is why we want a child memorialized and the name remembered. You can walk into any meeting of Compassionate Friends and see grieving parents who are wearing buttons with pictures of their children. Remember their names! Families of murdered children wear ribbons in their child's favorite color everywhere they go. Remember they lived! The most poignant part of the National Bombing Memorial in Oklahoma City are the small chairs sitting on the lawn, showing where in the building the babies were when the bomb snatched away their lives. Remember the pain!

There are many ways to physically honor and memorialize a life, but the most healing way is to fully discover what significance that life had on us. If we understand that value and that impact, what someone else thinks or remembers is not quite as important. We know what they meant. We carry their memories into the rest of our lives and create their history for them.

Decisions

The sixteen-year-old son of a former employee died of suicide. She cleaned out his room, gave away his clothes and most of his possessions and turned his room into an office within eight weeks of his death. She became friends with a woman whose sixteen-year-old son had died of suicide almost the same day as her son. Five years later that woman had not moved a single thing from her son's room. Both women did the right thing. They reacted in a way that fit them and their way of dealing with life and problems. Everyone must have permission to deal with these decisions in a way that fits them and gives them the most comfort.

I have often written that grief is like peeling an onion. It comes off one layer at a time and you cry a lot. If that analogy is accurate then perhaps it might be more healing for the clothes and the room to be something we gradually deal with and each step being a little of the onion being peeled. To do so all at once might be too dramatic and hanging on to everything for five years might indicate a lack of progress, but with that said, doing it differently does not mean it is wrong. It just means that is what fits that family.

Suicide

If grief is like peeling an onion, suicide shatters the onion and it seems like we must put it back together before we can grieve it. We are left with questions that can't be answered, reasons that can't be discovered or understood, and enough guilt and blame to make us doubt our own sanity. The grief following a suicide can last for years because the family is still searching for that one answer that can explain why their loved one made that decision on that day.

While there are no real absolute answers, there are some basic statements that might prove helpful.

There Is No One Cause

There is an old poem that says:
> *T'was the final straw that broke the camel's back*
> *then men noticed the fiendish pack*
> *but who among them ever saw*
> *the next to the last straw?*

Suicide is not the result of one thing someone said or did. We tend to look at the last thing that happened—a girlfriend broke up with him, a divorce was finalized, a crisis occurred at work, a failure in school—and think that is the one cause. Suicide happens because of a build-up of things, mostly hidden and unspoken, that makes the person vulnerable to being overwhelmed. That might be their basic personality or some chemical imbalance within their makeup. Whatever the cause, the load became too heavy to bear on that one day.

You Did Not Know Because They Did Not Want You to Know

Most of the time people contemplating ending their own lives are very secretive about their plans, and quite often, they seem to be better after the plans are finalized.

A man I was counseling with came to see me one morning. I was thrilled because he seemed so much better. He talked about plans for his future. We laughed together and parted as usual, not a hint of anything out of the ordinary. He left my office at 11:30 that morning and shot himself before 3:00 that afternoon. His plans were laid, the pressure was off, and he seemed to be at peace.

Suicide is an Issue to be Dealt With Not a Shame to be Hidden

The father of a dear friend of mine shot himself when she was a young woman over sixty years ago. He had terrible arthritis and there was very little that could alleviate the pain in those days. The family reacted as if some deep shame had come upon them and they refused to talk about it, even among themselves. She has spent her life in fear and apprehension. It is like there is a dark cloud hovering over her life and another tragedy could happen at any moment. They hid from what they perceived as shame, a blot on their family

The death of someone we know always reminds us that we are still alive—perhaps for some purpose which we ought to re-examine.
~Mignon McLaughlin, The Neurotic's Notebook, 1960

reputation, and were never allowed to grieve the loss and learn to cope with the death.

How a life ends does not define the life, nor does one act cast a shadow on the character of the person. This is not something to be ashamed of and, certainly, not something to be hidden and avoided. The fact that a loved one chose to end their life in this way does not place blame on the family or cast doubt upon the soul of the loved one.

DELAYED GRIEF

Then there are some grief experiences that seem to create a delay in the grieving process. Sometimes the cause is just a natural response to a particular situation, but sometimes the cause of the death forces us into a whirlwind of chaos that makes it impossible to deal with the grief until the situation and issues have been resolved. Perhaps exploring a few of these is the best way for us to understand that not all grieving experiences can be met or even faced on any normal time table.

Long-Time Caregiving

One of the more natural types of delayed grief can come at the end of a long and intense time of caregiving for a loved one. Often we are too exhausted to grieve and have no emotions left for the grieving. We often think that we have already grieved in anticipation of the death and therefore the job is complete.

When my father died, I did not feel anything. I was not as sad as I expected to be. I took care of all of the details and sat through the funeral like it was about someone else and not my father. I wondered if I had stopped loving my father. I wondered if I was such a cold person that I could not be touched even when my father died. I told myself that I had done anticipatory grief and had handled all of those feelings ahead of time. I told myself that, but it did not satisfy me nor did it seem to ring true.

I had been the primary caregiver to my father for many months. I was

If you suppress grief too much, it can well redouble.
~Moliere

the one who had to get up every morning, no matter what time I had flown in the night before, and put my father in the bathtub. I was the one who could never seem to rest fully and slept with one eye open expecting a call. I had no idea how exhausted and emotionally drained I was, nor did I connect my lack of feelings when he died to that condition of being emotionally drained and exhausted. I was also very busy with funeral and financial details as well as caring for my mother. Somehow I did not expect any of this to have any impact on whether or not I grieved when he died.

It took eight months for my father's death to become real to me, and eight months before I actually grieved that loss. I woke up late one night realizing what I had lost and found myself surprised by grief I thought was long gone.

Then I felt trapped. How do you explain why you are just now crying over the death of your father when you have been such a stoic for eight months? Like far too many others, I tried to hide my long delayed grief and just not talk about it until I finally could not hold it in any more and began to openly share my feelings of loss with my safe people who were shocked but, thankfully understood.

How many families have walked the long and lonely path caring for an Alzheimer's patient? They have had multiple losses along the way that they had to grieve—the loss of communication, the loss of history, the loss of motor ability, the loss of dignity—and some believe that when the death occurs that they should be done. But, for many, they have not yet even begun.

When a person is in the middle of day-to-day care, they have no time to reflect, to contemplate, to inventory the loss. The family and caregivers are in the trenches, in survival mode. So it takes quite some time afterward to reassemble the memories, to place them in context to the life and to finally be able to step back and see the complete picture. Then, and only then, can one adequately grieve the loss.

Grief With an Open End

I have often tried to imagine how a family could survive when a loved one has been taken and simply disappears from the face of the earth: no body is found, no one is ever charged in the disappearance, and no questions are ever answered. The grief is profound and overwhelming, of course, but it is also held in abeyance waiting for answers. There is an innate belief that if you grieve, then that means that you have lost hope that they might be found. The grief journey can never be complete until the person is either safely returned or the family has been able to put the body to rest.

Some of the same open-ended loss is experienced by the large number of families whose loved ones were pronounced missing and presumed dead as a result of war. How long can a family hope with nothing to sustain the hope? How long can they maintain the thought that their loved one is just lost in the jungle or in the desert and will someday be found?

The families of the victims of the terrorist attack on September 11 must live daily with a loved one going to work one morning and disappearing. They are just gone: no body to care for, no idea what they must have experienced, no way to say goodbye. For some, no grave or individual place where that person's life is honored and remembered.

Mass tragedies such as shootings, attacks, transportation wrecks also create an umbrella syndrome of "the victims' families". They become grouped together and all remembrances or ceremonies revolve around everyone who died. It is very difficult for a family to find the spotlight, to have their individual loved one's story told or mourned. This can delay or expand the grief because the family feels like they must work even harder to establish the significance of one life among many.

Open-ended grief must be made even more difficult as those who listen and try to help gradually fade away and few people even remember anymore. No one seems to notice the sadness of holidays, birthdays and anniversaries. Sometimes even the extended family seems to avoid and never bring it up again.

Grieving alone is grieving extended and deepened. Open-ended grief is just that, open-ended and never finished.

Death by Someone's Hand

When I speak of grief being delayed, I do not mean the sadness and tears are not there. They are not only there, they are overwhelming and devastating. There is no way to describe the pain or how helpless s person feels as they are unable to stop or control the tears. But the work of grief, the long journey towards a way to cope with the grief, is crushed under the load of the emotions and all of the walk toward healing is put on hold for a much later date.

This is especially true when a loved one is murdered. All these families can do is hurt and try to survive until the perpatrator is caught and the case is solved. They are grieving, of course, and need someone to walk with them and listen to them. But, chances are, any lessening of the pain or tears will be quite limited. The mind is dominated and fixated on finding the one who did this and seeing that they are properly punished. These grief journeys are extremely long and improvement is very slow.

Having the person charged does not free the family to think about anything else. The next hurdle is the trial, which adds to their frustration instead of bringing relief.

For the last fifteen years I have walked with a mother whose daughter was murdered. Recently she told me that when we first talked together I began explaining the concept of significance; that we needed to establish the significance of her daughter's life. She said she did not understand that until she had to sit through the trial. I remember sitting there as well. The attorney for the man who murdered her daughter went to great lengths trying to play on the sympathy of the jurors because of the very bad home life the young man had experienced. My friend said she was screaming inside, wanting to rise and tell the court who the guy had killed. She wanted them to know how wonderful her daughter was and how valuable she was, not only to her family, but to society itself. It was horrible to just sit there, knowing no one would tell her side of the story.

Victims' families become victims in our courtrooms. They have no rights. They cannot speak until the trial is over and then the speeches are limited or edited. I watched the state bring in a small busload of folks to stand as support for the murderer and take them to lunch each day at the state's expense, while the family of the victim sat on their own with no one to tell their story. Grief and justice sometimes do not live in the same room.

In my friend's case, it was a long time after the trial before we could do much more with her grief journey than cry and mourn the loss; too much anger to work through, too many questions that could not be answered, too much blame to be analyzed. I am sure some friends think she is wallowing in her grief and think I am not doing a very good job as her grief companion and guide. But this kind of loss is never gotten over. This kind of journey is never finished. She is coping better than I ever thought she could. That is something to be very proud about instead of judging how long it has taken. It takes as long as it takes, and no time limits are allowed.

Grieving What We Never Had

Sometimes we have to grieve what we never had, what we wish we had had. Not everyone who dies is a loving and accepting person. Cold and rejecting folks die as well. Some of these are mothers, fathers, siblings, family members, even our own children. Some people cannot gather at a gravesite to mourn the loss of a great love or the end of a beautiful friendship. Some must stand with mixed emotions, torn between the reality of the person being a part of their lives and family, but facing the fact that so much that was needed and longed for was missing and never found in the relationship.

Grieving what you never had but wished for is real grief and has a journey all its own. All the normal things we say about grief recovery may not help and may even make us feel worse. The usual outlets for sharing seem closed off to those trying to deal with a death following this kind of relationship. There is no way we could speak honestly of our feelings openly in a support group filled with people who are grieving the loss of a loving relationship. How could a person ever feel free to stand up in a meeting and say, "You folks were so fortunate to have had loving parents. My dad was a jerk."?

The journey has a different pattern and is fraught with side roads that can consume our time and energy and block us from finding healthy ways of dealing with this double loss grief.

Most of the time the relationships that produce this kind of loss come from dysfunctional families or families torn apart by substance or sexual abuse. More than just one person is impacted by the virulent personalities involved. Arguments between the surviving family members become almost inevitable. If a family is ever going to have a fight, they will have one about and around the funeral. Emotions are high and feelings are strained to the breaking point. Somebody says something, or makes a decision without consulting the rest of the family, and it is fireworks time.

I have seen families break apart during this experience, become almost warring camps and rarely, if ever, speak to each other again. The fact that they never find a way to deal with the hurts and losses in any constructive manner adds to the tragedy of a broken family.

If we allow ourselves to get caught up in these family issues, or if we allow ourselves to continue them past the funeral, we lock ourselves away from any chance of dealing with the loss or working through the hurts and rejections that make us grieve what we did not have instead of what we did have.

The first year is usually spent dealing with the family issues instead of our own response to the loss and our own grief. We seem to be constantly caught up in some argument over hurts and baggage that have been an ongoing struggle for what seems like forever. Then, perhaps, it comes time to divide up the property and a brand new war takes over the lives of the entire family. First thing you know, a year has passed and grieving is still sitting on the back burner.

Individual Agendas

Many of us have very private and personal issues that were never resolved before the person died. I still vividly remember a dear friend suddenly saying, "My dad is ill and it looks like he is going to die before we can deal with some agendas and I don't know that I can ever work through them if we don't". He did not explain the issue or even hint at its nature. Unfortunately my friend died in an accident before the death of his father, but I will never forget the sadness in his voice as he talked about the unfinished agendas he feared would never be faced.

It caused me to wonder how many other folks have family members who die with just such agendas unspoken and unmet. That has to leave a person with feelings of ambivalence when the family member or significant other dies. On the one hand they lived a life and, as such, should be honored. The rest of the family may not know the issue, so there must be a show of grief for their benefit, but what about the deep and hidden feelings of hurt and loss? What does one do with those?

AVOID BEING TRAPPED

The goal becomes finding ways to deal with our grief without being trapped in a never ending controversy or becoming a victim ourselves. There is no sure answer, of course. Each must face the task in their own way, but perhaps some suggestions might help.

Face the Realities

In a perfect world every hurt would be reconciled, every problem resolved and every grudge forgiven, but the world is far from perfect. In far too many cases the person dies without some wonderful experience of restoration. In far too many cases family members who have caused us pain or slight do not acknowledge their guilt or ask for forgiveness. We toss the word *forgiveness* around a lot but true forgiveness is an encounter that leads to healing and must be a mutual experience. Someone must want to be forgiven and someone must want to forgive. That is far too rare, so most of the time we are left with hurts that will not be fully resolved and we must chose whether these will become long term hurts that dominate our lives or something we will learn to cope with and move on.

Grief is perhaps an unknown territory for you. You might feel both helpless and hopeless without a sense of a 'map' for the journey. Confusion is the hallmark of a transition. To rebuild both your inner and outer world is a major project.
~Anne Grant

I do not know his name, but I admire a man whose loved one was killed in the Oklahoma City bombing. He was asked if he was going to the trial of the person who planted the bomb and he said, "No, and I don't even plan to read about it. That person has impacted my life as much as he is going to and I will not give him one more minute of my time".

One of my favorite stories is about a man who bought his newspaper at the same newsstand each morning. The operator of the stand was rude and insulted the man each morning. One day the man had a friend along who was astonished at the scene and asked the man why on earth did he buy his paper from that insulting person? The man answered, "Because I don't intend for that man to determine where I buy my paper". Sometimes it just gets down to who is going to govern our lives.

Discover the Values that Existed

I had a friend who chose to live in a very unsatisfying marriage. She stayed for the children and used me as an outlet for her anger and hurt. She would come to see me periodically and unload for about an hour on his latest antics and her feelings of inadequacy based on them. He died suddenly and, when I went to see her, she whispered in my ear, "All I can feel is relief".

She called a few months later and wanted to see me as soon as possible. When she came in she said, "I did not want you to hear from someone else that I was saying this, and I don't know how to tell you now, but I miss him." I assured her she was not going crazy and that I did not think her to be odd. I said, "Certainly you miss him. He was meeting some of your needs or you would never have stayed there. You miss having those needs met".

No one can meet all of our needs but, even in unsatisfactory relationships, some needs are being met. They may even be negative needs like the attention we get from others because we are suffering, but some needs are being met or we would be long gone. It might help to discover those needs and establish the value and significance of those and find other, perhaps healthier, ways to fulfill them.

Accept Responsibility

There are no one-sided problems. If we are manipulated, for example, we need to understand that manipulation is by invitation only. If we are manipulated it is partly because we have allowed it to happen. Our part may be that we were just too passive and afraid of conflict, which left the door open for more manipulation and pain. Recognizing that we do have some role is the first step away from becoming a long-term victim.

Talk About the Right Things

I tell people in marriage counseling to talk about their own needs instead of their mate's faults. Say, "Sometimes I feel so lonely and just need to be hugged," instead of, "You are cold and don't care about me". The same principle applies here. The person who hurt us is gone. The relationship we longed for can never happen. The things we needed from them are no longer a possibility. Cursing them, or the relationship, is an exercise in futility. It might get some attention for a time but over the long haul we become whining victims.

When we talk about it, perhaps it is better to talk about the needs we now have instead of the terrible person who caused them. "My childhood makes it hard for me to trust others and feel close, even though that is what I want". "My abuse has left me feeling vulnerable and afraid of relationships". These kinds of statements help your friends understand you and allow them to relate to you. Ranting and bemoaning how bad your father, mother, husband or others were makes them feel helpless. They can't do anything about the person who caused it, so they believe they have no way to be a comforting presence for you. But, when the hurts are focused on the present and what it will take to move forward, they can do much to help you overcome the impact that person made on your life.

Choose

Getting better is a choice. We can either spend our lives as victims looking for sympathy, or we can determine that we will face the issues, live through the pain, and find a new normal on the other side. We will not be totally victorious. There will be scars and it will always be easy for us to slip back into the abyss. But we are not going to be victims. The person or persons who hurt us will not win all of our lives. They will not dominate who we are or how we think.

LEARNING TO COPE

The aim of this book so far has been to simply show that grieving past the first year is not only normal but is very necessary, and, hopefully, giving permission to grieve without thinking something is wrong. There really is no end to grief. A chunk has been bitten from our hearts and it will not grow back. As long as we live, the loss will be with us. It will heal; it will leave a scar. Hopefully it will not dominate us, or cause the overwhelming grief we first experienced, but there will always be a nagging loss in our lives and, on occasion, something will trigger a fresh look at the loss.

The bottom line to grief is that our loved ones are no longer here and we are trying to learn how to live without their being here. We do not get well, we do turn the corner in the way we cope. That sounds like a one-time event. In reality there are many corner-turning times as we walk the grief journey. Some will be more dramatic, while others happen in the quiet stillness of our minds. Gradually we come to grips with the loss and learn to live with our loved ones in our hearts and in our memories.

There is no magic program that will guarantee a smooth

It's so curious: one can resist tears and 'behave' very well in the hardest hours of grief. But then someone makes you a friendly sign behind a window, or one notices that a flower that was in bud only yesterday has suddenly blossomed, or a letter slips from a drawer... and everything collapses.
~Colette

transition to coping. From my experience and from listening to scores of others, may I offer some suggestions that might help in that process?

The Power of Understanding

The last thing we want is for these feelings to be explained away or to be told we should forget them and move on. The most hurtful thing would be for them to be trivialized and made to seem unimportant. The bottom line to grieving is that we simply need to be understood. That is really what we are all looking for, just to find someone who will understand how and why we feel the way we feel. If we can be understood, we can move on. If we can't, we tend to park and get stuck in our grief journey.

I met a woman whose son was shot during a party. There was drinking involved and someone had a gun that somehow discharged and happened to take her son's life. She said she had a terrible struggle with the word *accident*. Somehow this seemed much more than an accident but she did not know what else to call it. She said every time she would tell someone of her struggle with the word they would say, "Well, do you think he was murdered?" She would stammer out that she did not think it was murder but it surely was more than an accident.

She finally went to see her son's friend who was at the party the night he was shot. She said:

> *The friend's name was John and he was a paraplegic. When I entered his room he was very defensive and had his hands clasped in front of him. I said, 'John, I am having a terrible time with the word accident. He lowered his hands, let out a deep sigh and said, 'So am I'. I began to heal at that very moment. It was like a tremendous load had been lifted off of me. I had found someone who understood what I was feeling and what I was trying to say.*

As time passes, more and more friends seem to grow tired of hearing about our loss, or perhaps they just feel so helpless and do not know what to say so they avoid us to protect themselves. The result is that it is much harder to find someone who understands us just at the time when we most need understanding and when we are most capable of explaining what we actually feel. My best advice is to not give up the search. Seek "safe" people. Safe people are those who seem comfortable with our pain, are willing to say the name of our loved one, and do not feel the need to explain or tell us how we should feel. Most of the time these will not come from family or our close friends. Usually those people are so anxious to make us feel better that they end up giving advice and sharing platitudes instead of listening. The best source may be a grief group where we can find others in circumstances like ours and we can do some mutual sharing. Or it might be someone who did not know your loved one and is willing to hear the stories for the first time. Safe people come in all shapes and sizes.

Even if we do not find that perfect safe person, we can get some understanding by being more specific when we talk. Instead of just saying, "I miss my loved one", say, "I missed her a lot this morning", or "I miss his touch every evening when we watched TV together", or "I miss the long talks we had", or "I miss the unconditional love she gave me". That sounds like a public pity party, but it isn't. Since we are willing to say it, it opens the door for a better response than the usual fluffy platitudes or uncomfortable head nodding and makes people feel more at ease. Hopefully they can respond by saying, "Mornings must seem pretty lonely for you right now" or "It's hard to watch TV by yourself, isn't it?" By having something specific to respond to, they do not feel as overwhelmed trying to answer your hurt. Even if they flunk the test totally, it helps us to have said it out loud. Grief works better out loud.

UNDERSTANDING OURSELVES

I wish I could promise every grieving soul a safe person who will listen and understand. Nothing is more healing than that. But those individuals and those experiences are rare and become rarer as time passes. At first we are almost overwhelmed by friends and family who say they want to help. Some of them might be safe and understanding, but far too many people think grief only lasts, at best, a few months so the listeners and those who understand fade away believing that they have done a good job because they were there at the right time. They don't understand that the right time is a long time.

One of the main reasons talking to a safe person helps is that we discover ourselves as we talk. Healing really is an inside job. We gain insight and understanding of ourselves in the process of telling our story to listening ears. Understanding ourselves is the first step toward learning to deal with our loss.

Since we might not have someone who will help, we can do the next best thing by writing out what we feel. Writing orders our minds. Writing makes us the safe person listening to ourselves. Many people find keeping a journal to be the best way to insure that they continue to write. For those who do not respond to that much detail or organization, just random notes telling what you are feeling at any given time will help. Keep the notes. Re-reading them should reveal a

We acquire the strength we have overcome.
~Ralph Waldo Emerson

pattern of thinking and feeling that can lead to a better understanding of what we feel and why we feel the way we do.

I love to lie in bed in the mornings and think things through. After my wife died this became my best time for trying to understand myself and my grief journey. I would try to honestly ask myself what I was thinking or feeling, how I was responding to what I was thinking or feeling, and why I was thinking and feeling the way I was at that time. I found I could have a good cry there in my bed and noticed that I often began to talk out loud about how much I missed her. I remember even almost screaming out at the sense of loss and loneliness. These sessions proved to be therapeutic to me. I was able to get a lot of built-up pressure off and say out loud what I wanted to say. I also began to understand myself and, even more important, accept myself. I gave myself permission to grieve. Maybe even better, I stopped taking my own grief away from me.

The Blame Game

The turning point in the process of growing up is when you discover the core of strength within you that survives all hurt.

When bad things happen to us the normal, and almost automatic, reaction is to figure out what or who to blame. We live in a cause and effect world so there must be a reason for everything that happens to us, good or bad. Many of us find it scary to think of a world where things happen without some set cause. Thinking that a certain number of people are going to have cancer or be victims of an accident and that the percentages of those events do not distinguish between good and bad, rich or poor, religious or non-religious seems to be threatening to most of us.

It is almost inevitable then that at some point on the grief journey we will begin trying to place the blame:

This happened because. . .
It is my fault
Why didn't I. . .
Why did God let this happen?

These questions express feelings we could call anger. Not anger as in mad or throwing temper tantrums, but anger that comes from deep hurts and frustrations. These feelings are normal of course and do not need to become a problem unless they become obsessions to us. The problem is these feelings do not float well. They need a place to focus and where they focus can become a problem.

Most of the places of focus are logical and will normally work themselves out or can be worked through. Sometimes the anger focuses on doctors, hospitals, friends, churches and pastors, extended family members—anyone we perceive as failing us in our time of sorrow.

Swallowed anger creates depression. Anger needs to be expressed. Talk about what you feel. Do so even if no one seems to understand. Talking relieves the pressure and helps us gradually discover what is really going on inside of us.

Anyone who has watched those TV shows such as *Hoarders* or *Intervention* knows that these individuals are desperately ill and have psychological and physical addictions that are destroying their lives. But, the most interesting part of each episode is when the person describes their past, their history, their journey. Every one of them will recount a trauma, a loss, a grieving experience that was the trigger. "I was fine until..." It might be a death, a divorce, an abusive situation, an attack. Whatever it was, the anger was too big to handle and so they either started self-medicating or covering themselves up with stuff until they could no longer safely walk through their houses. It always begins with hurt and with anger that is swallowed and turned inward.

When the person is allowed and encouraged to focus on the loss or the trauma, rather than the resulting behavior, healing can be quick and dramatic. Family members allow the hurt to be discussed, explored and resolved rather than complaining about the substance abuse or a house that is falling down from hoarding. Words matter, and giving voice to internal struggles can be powerful.

Sometimes doing something physical helps. Walking, running, playing a sport, practicing yoga, hitting a pillow, screaming, crying and expressing anger with the strongest language you are comfortable with can all give an outlet to those feelings. It needs to come out. If it is swallowed, it becomes depression.

RE-REMEMBER

Too often, when a person says that they are struggling with their grief—they are stuck, they just can't move on—it can be traced back to the funeral experience. Some people choose not to have any type of service because they think that it is easier not to go through the gathering and the emotions. Some people have very perfunctory or impersonal services that do nothing to honor the life or to embrace the grief of those left behind. Some people have very harmful services where the loved one's death was used as a vehicle for evangelizing or judging.

None of these provide those important first steps on the grief path and people can find themselves still wandering around at the beginning, unsure and unprepared for the long journey ahead.

I visited with a funeral director who had lost her sixteen-year-old son in a car accident. She explained that she had gone to a minister that she knew well in her town and asked him to conduct the funeral. She told him that her son was spiritual but not a churchgoer. That he was a seeker. That he was still a teenager trying to figure out where he fit in this life, just like all kids his age. She asked the minister to honor his life, to talk about his gifts and what the world had lost from his promising future.

The minister agreed, but, unfortunately, failed. His opening words at the service were, "Shawn

*Memory is
a way of holding
onto the
things you love,
the things you are,
the things you never
want to lose.*
~From the television show
The Wonder Years

was a lost soul." He judged this young life rather than celebrated it. It destroyed this mother and, ten years after the fact, she sobbed as she recounted her story. Ten years later it was still a fresh wound and a fresh loss because she was not given the support and strength she needed from the beginning. She couldn't begin the process of placing his life in her memories because the memories had been ignored.

One suggestion that might be worth considering is, have another service. Re-remember: gather family and friends together on a special day such as the birthday, the anniversary of the death, a holiday and have another time together. Wipe the old memories of a service that harmed or meant nothing and create new paths together. Light candles, play music, show pictures and tell the stories once again. This is exactly what I told this mother. I offered to come to her town and help her put something together because we believe so strongly in the healing power of ceremony.

Oftentimes tragic deaths, such as substance abuse or suicide, are ignored during the funeral because no one quite knows how to address the issue, so it becomes the elephant in the room that everyone dances around. The family is left to their own devices in trying to find companions on the grief journey because everyone is too afraid to say anything. Finding a Celebrant, or a clergy person, or a friend who you believe can express the loss in a safe, healing and honest way, and gathering again to have the type of service that supports the grieving experience rather than stunts it is one of the most important choices you can make.

Sometimes the family chooses to scatter the cremated remains, either because it was the loved one's wishes or they thought it represented a fitting tribute to the life. Or, the urn is sitting on someone's mantle because no one could quite make the decision what should be done. However, later, many people realize that having a special place where that life is memorialized is valuable and important in their grieving experience. It can be a vital part of the grief journey to have a sacred spot, a place for honoring the life.

If you are in that situation, you might consider making your own spot. Plant a garden or a tree, buy a bench, place the urn in a niche at a cemetery and have a ceremony again to commemorate the life and the memories. It's never too late to have a tribute again, or for the first time.

MEMORIES

My wife loved to watch the big horse races. She only went to two races in her life and never bet a single penny on any of them, but, when it was time for those races, she suddenly knew which horses were running and had her own personal favorite, picked more by the name or the color of the jockey's shirt than by any odds offered by the experts.

This year I watched the Belmont. Memories flooded into my mind and heart. Even though it has been four years since she died, it was almost like she was there sitting beside me as I watched a horse win the 2015 Triple Crown. One memory led to another and suddenly I was reliving some wonderful times we had shared together. The car trips we took all across the United States and Canada, when we would drive for days and never turn on the radio because that would interfere with our talking. I realized again that if I had a problem it was not over until I talked to her about it. She was not just my best friend she was the only one in her class. I had friends, close friends, and then I had Barbara, and I realized how much that meant. I thought of the intimacy we shared and the joy brought by being close. I could almost feel the surge of peace that came when we held each other close. I got so lost in memories I almost missed the race. When I jerked back to the present I noticed I was smiling and feeling such a surge of gratitude for all we had and all she meant,

She was no longer wrestling with the grief, but could sit down with it as a lasting companion and make it a sharer in her thoughts.
~George Eliot

If I had watched that same race four years ago I would not have been able to see it for the tears in my eyes. I could not have managed reliving those very same memories without a breakdown, and I would have been depressed for days on end. Those were the memories that hurt the most. Those were the things I hated the most to lose. When a wave of grief hit me, it was caused by those very things that I knew I would never have again and did not know how I could live without. The losses I dreaded the most and were the hardest to think about, now were the memories I enjoyed the most.

Maybe that is what is meant when they say we do not get over our grief but we do turn the corner in the way we cope. I am not over my grief and I never will be. I will never have another friend like my wife. I will never have another companion I can enjoy in that special way. I will never feel the peace I felt when she was around or the support I felt as she sat on the front row while I gave a speech and laughed at the jokes like it was the first time she ever heard them. That will never come back. But gradually the pain of remembering those losses has become the joy of remembering and reliving them.

That did not happen quickly or automatically. It was a struggle. I did not want to feel good again. I did not want to get better. I wanted to go off in a cave somewhere and have pity parties for the rest of my life.

I really think there comes a time when we must say, "Okay this has happened to me. Now do I let it take my life away, or do I surrender to the reality and figure out how to live in my new reality?" I am not sure that is a set time or even a conscious decision. I do not remember any dramatic experience but, somehow, gradual change began to move me toward enjoying what I used to have, instead of being crushed by it.

I think the key to that movement is *gratitude.* In my experience, the folks who learn to cope the best are the ones who develop a sense of gratitude. I don't know whether the memories create the gratitude or the gratitude creates the memories, but I do know that being grateful for all we had turned what would have been an out-of-control hurting session and days of depression into a wonderful afternoon of memories.

Grief is a Journey

We move from seeing the person by sight
To seeing them in memories.
Memories are also in constant motion
At first they are too painful for endurance,
and every memory breaks our hearts.

Gradually they help us establish the significance
of our love and of our loss
In time memories become our most precious possession.
The ones that once hurt the most become the ones
we never tire of telling.

Over time the memories wrap themselves around our being.
And our loved one is reborn inside of our hearts.
That is called the

Journey of Grief

~Doug Manning

About the Author

Doug Manning

Doug's career has included minister, counselor, business executive, author and publisher. He and his wife, Barbara, were parents to four daughters and long-term caregivers to three parents.

After thirty years in the ministry, Doug began a new career in 1982 and has devoted his time to writing, counseling and leading seminars in the areas of grief and elder care. His publishing company, InSight Books, Inc., specializes in books, video and audio productions specifically designed to help people face some of the toughest challenges of life.

Doug has a warm, conversational style in which he shares insights from his various experiences. Sitting down to read a book from Doug is like having a long conversation with a good friend.

Selected Resources from InSight Books

By Doug Manning

The Back Nine: Life Beyond Retirement*
Building Memories: Planning a Meaningful Funeral
Journey of Grief DVD**
Lean On Me Gently: Helping the Grieving Child*
The Power of Presence: Helping People Help People Book or DVD
Sacred Moments: A Minister Speaks About Funerals
Special Care Series
Thoughts for the Holidays*
Thoughts for the Lonely Nights book/journal or CD
Thoughts for the Grieving Christian book/journal or CD
Spanish: *Spanish Special Care* books or *Grief Care Series* CD set

Other Resources from InSight Books

I Know Someone Who Died coloring book by Connie Manning
The Empty Chair: The Journey of Grief After Suicide* e-Book
    by Beryl Glover (only available as an e-Book)
Memories Too Few: A Letter to Parents About Pregnancy Loss*
    by Kathy Manning Burns
Comfort Cards bereavement card collection

* Also available as e-Books from your favorite e-Book vendor
** Also available streaming on Amazon

For a complete catalog or ordering information contact:

InSight Books, Inc.
800.658.9262 or 405.810.9501
OrdersAndInfo@InSightBooks.com
www.InsightBooks.com

Funeral Homes in the U.S. and Canada may also order InSight products from The Dodge Company